Blake left his seat. He walked back to Rosa, grabbed her coat sleeve, and led her to the front door. There was an empty seat by the door. Rosa dropped her purse. Instead of just leaning over to get it, she sat on the "white" seat to pick it up.

"Get off my bus," Blake said. He was growing angrier.

"I will get off," Rosa replied. Blake was a tall, strong man. By now he was leaning over her in a threatening way. His fists were clenched. Rosa did not look afraid. She did not raise her voice. She just said, in a quiet, clear voice, "I know one thing. You better not hit me."

Rosa Parks
AND THE BUS
TO FREEDOM

BETH JOHNSON

Rosa Parks
and the Bus to Freedom

TP **THE TOWNSEND LIBRARY**

For more titles in the Townsend Library,
visit our website: **www.townsendpress.com**

Copyright © 2012 by Townsend Press, Inc.
Printed in the United States of America

9 8 7 6 5 4 3 2 1

Cover illustration © 2012 by Hal Taylor

Townsend Press, Inc.
439 Kelley Drive
West Berlin, NJ 08091
permissions@townsendpress.com

ISBN-13: 978-1-59194-288-7
ISBN-10: 1-59194-288-8

Library of Congress Control Number:
2012933720

CONTENTS

Introduction 1

Chapter 1 5

Chapter 2 13

Chapter 3 20

Chapter 4 25

Chapter 5 32

Chapter 6 35

Chapter 7 42

Chapter 8 48

Chapter 9 52

Chapter 10 55

Chapter 11 63

INTRODUCTION

It was Thursday, December 1, 1955. Rosa Parks left her job at 5 o'clock. She wasn't feeling her best. She had bursitis, a painful swelling of the joints. Her feet hurt badly.

There was a big crowd at the bus stop. Because black people had to sit in the last ten rows of the bus, she knew if the bus was crowded, she would have to stand all the way home. She decided to do some Christmas shopping while she waited for the crowd to thin out.

Later, carrying her shopping bag,

Rosa climbed onto an emptier bus. She found a seat in a row about two-thirds of the way back where three other black passengers were sitting. It felt good to get off her aching feet and to put her shopping bag down.

At the next stop, a number of white people boarded the bus. After they found seats, one white man was left standing.

The bus driver turned around and looked at his black passengers. For the first time, Rosa noticed his face. She realized that it was a driver named James Blake. She remembered James Blake all too well. Twelve years earlier, he had forced her off his bus when she tried to walk through the "whites only" section of the bus to get to a seat in the back.

Blake walked down the aisle. Looking directly at Rosa, he said, "Move, y'all. I want those seats."

There was only one white man

waiting for a seat. But on the segregated buses, a row had to be either "black" or "white." All four black people in the row would have to move.

For a moment, nobody moved. Blake raised his voice. "Y'all make it light on yourselves and let me have those seats," he said again.

The two black women sitting across the aisle got up and moved to the rear of the bus. Then the man sitting by the window, beside Rosa, began to rise. Rosa swung her legs aside so that he could get out.

And then she moved into the empty window seat. Turning her back on Blake, she looked out the window.

Rosa Parks had had enough. She was tired, and her feet hurt. She was going to keep her seat.

Blake said, "Look, woman. I told you I want that seat. Are you going to stand up?"

Rosa said, "No, I am not."

"Then I'm going to call the police and have you arrested," Blake said.

Rosa quietly replied, "You may do that."

And in that moment of quiet defiance, Rosa Parks took the first step in the march that would change the course of history forever.

To understand why Rosa took this courageous stand, it's important to understand the times she lived in and how she was raised.

CHAPTER 1

Rosa Parks was born Rosa Louise McCauley on February 4, 1913, in Tuskegee, Alabama. Her parents were James and Leona McCauley. James was a carpenter. Leona was a teacher.

Tuskegee had been an important city in black American history for a long time. It was the home of Booker T. Washington, the famous black educator who started Tuskegee University in 1881. For many years, the university was the best place in America for black students to get an education. Another famous black American, George Washington Carver, was a teacher at Tuskegee. Carver was an amazing inventor and scientist. He developed more than 300 products from the peanut and 175 from the sweet potato.

One day, Rosa Parks' name would be as well known as Washington's and Carver's. But that would have seemed unlikely when Rosa was growing up. She was just a little girl who was sick a lot. Her tonsils, lumps of tissue in the back of the throat, were often sore and swollen. When her throat hurt, it was hard for her to eat. Because of her bad health, she was small and thin. In fact, although her little brother Sylvester was two years younger, Rosa was smaller than he was for much of their childhood.

There is a family story about Rosa and her childhood sickness. When she was two and a half, her grandfather took her to see the doctor about her tonsils.

As young as she was, she sat up very straight and let the doctor look down her throat without fussing or crying. The doctor praised her for being a brave little girl. Maybe this was a hint of the courage Rosa was going to show later in her life!

By the time of that visit to the doctor, Rosa and her family had moved from Tuskegee to the tiny town of Pine Level, Alabama. There they lived with Leona's parents on their farm. Because James was often away for long periods, building houses in other towns, Leona needed her parents' help to care for the two children. After a while, James stopped coming home at all. From the time she was five until she was an adult, Rosa did not see her father. Leona began teaching school in a town miles away. She had no car, so she had to stay away all week. As a result, Rosa was raised mostly by her grandparents.

Rosa's grandparents were very important in her life. In their different ways, they both taught her what it meant to be a black person in the South in the early 20th century.

Grandfather Sylvester had been born a slave on an Alabama plantation, a large farm where crops, such as cotton, were grown to be sold. In the South before the Civil War (1861–1865), plantations were worked mostly by slaves. His mother was also a slave, but his father was a white man—in fact, he was the owner of the plantation. Slaves like Grandfather's mother did not have any rights. They were considered property, just like a horse or a wagon. If a slave owner wanted to have children with a female slave, there was nothing she could do about it. If she said "No," she could be beaten, sold, or even killed. So on plantations, it was not unusual to see slave children who were of mixed race.

Like many of these children, Grandfather Sylvester had very light skin and straight hair.

You might think that a plantation owner would treat his own children better than the other slaves. But the opposite was often true. Owners felt embarrassed to see slaves growing up who looked like them. Everyone who saw those light-skinned children knew that the owners had taken advantage of the children's mothers. Owners' wives were angry to see children that their husbands had fathered with other women. As a result, the half-white slaves might be treated even worse than the black slaves.

That was the case with Grandfather Sylvester. As he was growing up, he was beaten and starved by his white owners. He grew to hate white people. He talked to Rosa about how whites had mistreated him. He warned her that white people were no good, and that she should stay away from them. He didn't even like it when Rosa played with the white children on the neighboring farm, or went fishing with the elderly white woman who lived nearby.

Grandfather had his own ways of getting back at white people. In the South, there were very strict rules about how blacks were supposed to behave around whites. Blacks were expected to act very respectful. They were supposed to call everyone "Mr." or "Mrs." They were supposed to step off the sidewalk to let a white person pass by. They were never supposed to touch a white person. But Grandfather looked like a white man. So when he was in a place where people did not know him, he would break all the rules. He would walk down the sidewalk with whites. He would call white men by their first names and shake hands with them. Then he would laugh behind their backs, knowing how angry they would be if they knew he was black.

Like her husband, Grandmother Rose was half white. Her mother had been a slave, and her father had been a white servant on the same plantation. As a young woman, Grandmother Rose took care of the white plantation owners' baby.

Unlike black slaves, white servants were paid for their work. So, when Grandmother's father had saved enough money, he bought 12 acres of the plantation. Later, the white child that Grandmother had helped raise gave her six more acres as a gift. Those 18 acres made up the little farm that Rosa lived on with her grandparents. Grandmother knew that the way black people were treated in the South was not fair or right. But her experiences with white people had not all been bad. She was not bitter and angry towards all whites in the way her husband was.

Little Rosa loved her grandparents. She listened to both of them. She understood her grandfather's anger. She admired his outspoken ways. At the same time, she respected the way her grandmother was open-minded about people. As Rosa grew up, it was clear she had learned both her grandparents' lessons well.

CHAPTER 2

Rosa Parks' story really begins much earlier in American history, at the time of the Civil War in the 1860s.

The main cause of the American Civil War was a dispute between the North and South over slavery. The economy (the way of making and managing money) of the Southern states was based on slavery. The South had many large plantations that needed cheap workers—in other words, slaves. Without slaves, the entire Southern economy would fall apart.

But it wasn't only money that the South was fighting for. Many white Southerners, even those who didn't own slaves (and most didn't), were angry that the United States government should meddle in their way of life. They had grown up believing that slavery was right. They even believed that God approved of slavery. When some people said that the slaves must be freed, those Southerners were as outraged as if someone had taken away their homes.

In 1865, when the Civil War ended, slavery became illegal. But the change in law did not change people's hearts. Many white Southerners were not ready to treat black people as equals. Angry and bitter, they looked for ways to keep blacks down. Organizations like the Ku Klux Klan became popular. The Klan, or KKK, is a terrorist group that promotes "white power." Klan members wearing white robes and masks rode through the countryside on horses, threatening black Americans. Sometimes they claimed to be the ghosts of Southern soldiers who had died in the Civil War. They burned black homes and businesses. They tortured and killed people in order to keep the black community frightened.

Racists also used what were called "Jim Crow laws" to keep black people down and deprive them of their basic human dignity. "Jim Crow" laws touched on almost every part of everyday life and firmly established segregation—separation of the races—as a way of life in the South for many years to come. This policy of segregation applied to public schools, public places and transportation, restaurants, and drinking fountains. Even public bathrooms had signs reading "Whites Only" and "Colored Only." A black person attempting to enter a whites-only area would take a tremendous risk;

he could be arrested, beaten, or worse.

In addition to affecting the day-to-day life of blacks, "Jim Crow" laws also made it almost impossible for blacks to exercise their right to vote. For one thing, offices where blacks could register to vote were rarely open. Their hours weren't advertised. When an office was open and a number of people had lined up to register, the office would suddenly close.

Also, blacks had to pass a test and pay a tax in order to register. But the tests were scored by white people who never told the blacks why they had supposedly "failed." On those tests, blacks were required to answer questions that were sometimes ridiculous, such as, "How many bubbles are there in a bar of soap?" Other times the questions were impossibly difficult, such as "Recite the entire U.S. Constitution."

As a little girl in Pine Level, Rosa

probably didn't know much about the Civil War or the reasons behind the Jim Crow laws. But she knew about the Ku Klux Klan. After all, her Grandfather Sylvester was known as an "uppity" black man who refused to bow down to whites. He and Grandmother Rose were the only black people in Pine Level who owned land. One of Rosa's first memories was of her grandfather sitting on the front porch all night, holding his shotgun in case the Klan came by. Many nights, little Rosa would sit up with him. She said later that if there was going to be any shooting, she wanted to see it.

There was a reason the Klan was especially nervous when Rosa was a little girl. World War I was ending, and black American soldiers were coming home from fighting in Europe. The soldiers had served bravely. In Europe, they had been greeted as heroes and shown respect by white people. Now back in their own country, those same men were being treated as second-class citizens. They could not eat in white restaurants. They could not stay in white hotels. They had to drink from "colored" water fountains. They could be workers, but never bosses. They weren't allowed to buy homes in white neighborhoods. Their children had to attend second-rate black schools. White people, even white children, called them "boy" and even more insulting names.

Older black people were used to being treated this way. Many of them had the attitude, "That's just the way things are." But it was different for these young soldiers. They had experienced another kind of life, one in which they weren't judged by the color of their skin. They wanted that kind of life in their own communities. They began speaking out. Stories in black newspapers demanded better treatment for blacks. More and more people joined civil rights organizations, especially the National Association for the Advancement of Colored People (NAACP).

As Southern blacks spoke up for themselves, Southern whites became more angry. The most vicious whites carried out horrible attacks called "lynchings," in which they tortured black people to death and hung their bodies from trees. In Pine Level, as in many towns, Rosa and her classmates brought their books home from school every day. They were afraid the Klan would burn the school during the night.

This was the atmosphere that Rosa grew up in.

CHAPTER 3

Pine Level was a very tiny town. In fact, some people would say it didn't deserve to be called a town at all. It consisted of a gravel road and three small general stores. One of those stores contained the post office. Although there were two schools—one black, one white—there were not many other obvious signs of segregation.

Rosa and her little brother Sylvester attended the same black school that their mother had gone to when she was a little girl. Pine Level School was a small wooden building with only one room and only one teacher. All 60 students, from first grade through sixth grade, met there in the single room.

Rosa and Sylvester walked to school every day. The white children rode a bus to their school, which was a modern brick building. Sometimes white kids would throw trash out the bus windows at the black children. Rosa told Sylvester to ignore the rude behavior. But one time she couldn't ignore it herself. A white boy named Franklin met Rosa and Sylvester on the road. He began calling them names, then made a fist as if he were going to hit Rosa. Rosa picked up a brick and said she would hit him back. Franklin backed off.

Rosa went home and proudly told her grandmother that she had stood up to Franklin. Instead of being pleased, her grandmother scolded her. She told Rosa that threatening to hit a white person was a dangerous thing to do. Grandma Rose said, "If you act like that, you'll get lynched before you're twenty!"

Mostly, though, Rosa was not a little girl who got into trouble. In fact, the other children sometimes teased her for being a "prissy little lady." She was shy, polite, and soft-spoken. Even though she lived on a farm and spent much of her time running around barefoot, she loved dressing up when she had the chance. She liked to wear little white gloves and shiny shoes when she went to church.

But dressing-up days were few. Most of the time, Rosa and her family worked very hard on their farm. The family didn't have much money, but they did produce most of their own food. They raised chickens and vegetables. They had their own walnut, pecan, and fruit trees.

When Rosa was seven, she began

making extra money for the family by picking cotton on a white neighbor's plantation. Many other black children did the same. Later in her life, Rosa told people that the cotton pickers worked "from can to can't." She meant they worked from sunrise, when you "can" see, until sunset, when you "can't." Picking cotton was hard work. The temperature often rose over 100 degrees. The children's bare feet would get blistered by the hot, sandy soil. When the blisters got too painful, the children would work on their knees. The pickers' hands would get cut by the dried bristles on the cotton plants. When that happened, they had to be very careful. If they got blood on the white cotton, the boss would whip them.

But whippings were not a big part of Rosa's life. For the most part, her life with her grandparents in Pine Level was ordinary, at least for a little black girl in the Jim Crow South. Nobody yet imagined that Rosa was going to become a very *extra*ordinary person.

CHAPTER 4

In 1924, when Rosa was 11, the Pine Level school closed. For most local black children, that was the end of their education. But Rosa's mother, Leona, was determined that Rosa should get more schooling. Leona was still teaching in a town far away from Pine Level. She took a second job as a maid in order to send Rosa to a private school.

To attend her new school, Rosa had to move 25 miles from Pine Level to Montgomery, the capital of Alabama. There, she lived with an aunt. Her new school's name was the Montgomery Industrial School. But Rosa and everybody else called it "Miss White's school."

Miss White's school was an unusual one. Its 250 students were all black girls. But its founder, Alice White, and all its teachers were white women from up North. They had come to Alabama because they believed black children deserved as good an education as white children. Very few Southern white teachers were willing to teach black students. In fact, Miss White and her teachers were disliked by many white people in Montgomery. Some of these people told them to go back to the North and mind their own business. Racists burned the school twice, but Miss White rebuilt it both times.

At Miss White's school, Rosa and the other girls were taught English and science. They also learned practical skills, including cooking and sewing. Rosa loved sewing and was soon making most of her own clothes. Miss White's students also spent a lot of time learning about Christianity and "proper" behavior. Every school day included time for prayers and Bible study. The girls were not allowed to dance, wear big earrings, straighten their hair, put on bright lipstick, or even go to the movies. Some girls rebelled against these rules, but Rosa approved of them. She was still a "little lady" who valued being neat, kind, and respectful.

Rosa fit in right away. Years later she said, "I liked going to school at Miss White's. It was not hard for me to adjust to being taught by white teachers, because I had learned back in Pine Level, especially from the old woman who used to take me fishing, that white people could treat you like a regular person."

But living in the big city of Montgomery was a shock for Rosa. In tiny, rural Pine Level, there weren't any public facilities such as libraries, restaurants, or hotels. While white people and black people didn't mix much, there weren't many signs of official segregation.

But Montgomery was different. There, for the first time, Rosa saw "Whites Only" signs everywhere. There were white restrooms and black restrooms; white restaurants and black restaurants; white phone booths and black phone booths; white libraries and black libraries. Public swimming pools were for whites only. Trains and buses had white sections and black sections. Movie theaters had separate entrances for white people and black people, and blacks had to sit in the balcony. Rosa noticed that facilities for whites were new and clean. Areas for blacks tended to be old and run-down.

Years later, Rosa remembered noticing the "whites only" and "colored" drinking fountains. She wondered if "white water" tasted different.

Sometimes the rules of segregation were hard to figure out. One hot summer afternoon, Rosa and her cousin Annie Mae walked into a store that had a lunch counter. They each asked for a soda pop. The white waitress told them that she couldn't sell them soda. She suggested that they buy ice cream cones instead.

Rosa didn't understand. Why couldn't they have soda? Finally she got it. Because soda came in a glass, the girls would have to sit down to drink it. Black people weren't allowed to sit in the restaurant. But the waitress *could* sell them ice cream cones, which they would have to carry outside to eat.

Other times, segregation led to

situations that were just plain ridiculous. A few years later, when Rosa was a young woman, it became the "in" thing for wealthy white men and women to get suntans. As a result, some white people were darker than light-skinned people who were considered black—people like Rosa's grandfather. Business owners whose customers were white became worried. What if they accidentally let in "black" customers while kicking out suntanned "whites"? In Washington, D.C., some hotel owners actually hired "race experts" to stand in the lobbies and try to figure out who was black and who was white!

As Rosa spent more time in Montgomery, she became used to the rules of segregation. On the outside, she did not show how much those rules bothered her. But she found ways to express her feelings privately. For instance, as she grew older, she refused to drink from "colored" water fountains. No matter how thirsty she was, she would wait until she was in a place where she could get a drink and not feel insulted. She refused to use "colored" elevators; instead, she would use the stairs. In small, quiet ways, Rosa was becoming a rebel.

CHAPTER 5

Finally, the pressure against Miss White's school grew to be too much. In 1928, Alice White announced that she was closing the school. By then she was elderly, blind, and in poor health. And it had become too hard to get Northern teachers to come to a city where they would be criticized and even threatened.

Rosa was deeply disappointed. She had spent three years at Miss White's and had finished eighth grade. When her mother had trouble paying the tuition, Rosa began cleaning classrooms to cover the fees. For the rest of her life, she would praise the education she received at Miss White's. As an old lady, she told an interviewer, "What I learned best at Miss White's was that I was a person with dignity and self-respect, and that I should not set my sights lower than anybody else just because I was black."

Rosa transferred to another school, where she finished tenth grade and started eleventh. But then bad news arrived from Pine Level. Rosa's grandmother, Rose, was very ill. Her Grandfather Sylvester had died some years earlier. Her little brother was working full time. With her mother, Leona, teaching school in a distant town, Rosa felt it was her duty to go home to care for her grandmother. She quit school and moved back to Pine Level.

After a month, Grandmother Rose died, and Rosa returned to Montgomery.

She started eleventh grade again, but this time it was her mother, Leona, who became ill. Again Rosa left school and went home. She wasn't happy about quitting school, but she didn't complain, either. She said, "It was just something that had to be done."

For the next several years, Rosa took care of the farm and sometimes worked cleaning people's homes. She lived a quiet life. But an important—and unexpected—visitor was just around the corner.

CHAPTER 6

When Rosa first met Raymond Parks, she didn't like him much.

"He was too white," she said bluntly. Although she had loved her light-skinned grandfather, she found dark-skinned men more attractive. And Raymond Parks was very light. Except for his hair, he could have passed for white.

When the two met, Rosa was 18 and Parks was 28. (Everybody, including Rosa, called him by his last name.) He was a barber in Montgomery. A mutual friend, who knew Parks had recently broken up with his girlfriend, introduced the two. At their first meeting, Rosa was polite, but she made it clear she wasn't interested in romance.

Still, Parks didn't give up. He soon drove out to Pine Level to call on Rosa. Finding her wasn't easy. The family didn't have a telephone, and he didn't have her address. He stopped to ask an elderly black neighbor if she knew Rosa. The neighbor thought he was a white man, so she said no!

Eventually Parks found his way to Rosa's house. He visited with her and her mother. The next week he came back. When she saw him coming, Rosa went to her room and pretended to be sleeping until he left. But finally Parks convinced Rosa to come out with him. He had bait that she couldn't resist—a jazzy little red sports car.

"It was something very special for

a young black man to own his own car, particularly when he wasn't driving for any of the white folks," Rosa later said.

Once Rosa gave Parks a chance, she discovered that he was a remarkable man. He didn't have any formal education. He'd grown up in an area where there were no black schools, so his mother had taught him to read and write at home. Still, he had become an eager reader who had educated himself on many topics. Working as a barber had added to his knowledge and interests. In the segregated South, the black barbershop was an important community center. Along with the black church, it was one of the few public places where groups of blacks could gather, talk, and exchange news without being overheard by whites.

The thing that impressed Rosa most, though, was that Parks was an activist. He didn't just talk about the unfair ways that blacks were treated. He worked to change things. For many years, he'd been a member of the National Association for the Advancement of Colored People—the NAACP.

At the time that Parks and Rosa met, the NAACP was involved in an important case known as "the Scottsboro Boys." The Scottsboro Boys were nine young men, ages 12 to 18, who had been accused of raping two white women. The case against them was very weak. In fact, it was unlikely that anything at all had happened to the two women. But this was a time and place where a black man could be lynched for just looking at a white woman. After a hasty trial before an all-white jury, eight of the nine Scottsboro Boys were sentenced to die in the electric chair.

Parks was a founding member of the National Committee to Defend the Scottsboro Boys. He and other activists spent many hours raising money for the young men's defense, hiring lawyers for them, and spreading the news about the way the men had been framed.

Rosa deeply admired Parks for getting involved in the case. She wanted to attend meetings with him, but he said no. The work he was doing was very dangerous. The committee met in secret, knowing that the police were looking for excuses to raid them. Members were accused of being Communists, traitors, and troublemakers. To protect her from knowing too much, Parks wouldn't even tell Rosa the names of the other men on the committee. He jokingly told her they were all named Larry.

In Parks, Rosa found someone who was as fiery and outspoken as her grandfather had been. She said, "He was the first man of our race, aside from my grandfather, with whom I actually discussed anything about the racial conditions. And he was the first, aside from my grandfather . . . who was never actually afraid of white people. So many African Americans felt that you just had to be under Mr. Charlie's heel— that's what we called the white man, Mr. Charlie—and couldn't do anything to cross him. In other words, Parks believed in being a man and expected to be treated as a man."

Rosa's opinion of Parks had changed forever. In 1932, when Rosa was 20, they were married and moved into an apartment in Montgomery.

In spite of the hard work by Parks and many others, the case of the Scottsboro Boys was not settled for a long time. In 1933, after one of the two women who had claimed to be raped admitted that she had lied, the men were given a new trial. Another all-white jury again condemned them to die. At that point, the Supreme Court got involved. They said the trial hadn't been fair because no blacks had been allowed on the jury. In 1937, the four youngest men were freed. But the last of the Scottsboro Boys wasn't released from prison until 1950. That was nineteen years after the supposed crime had happened.

The case of the Scottsboro Boys, and Parks' example, changed Rosa Parks' life. She had always known that the way black people were treated was wrong. Now she began to think about how to put her beliefs into action.

CHAPTER 7

After they settled in Montgomery, Parks encouraged Rosa to finish her high-school education. She returned to school and earned her diploma. Parks went on working as a barber, and Rosa took in sewing and worked as an aide at a hospital.

Then Rosa found a better job as a secretary at Maxwell Field, a nearby military base. World War II had begun, and many extra workers were needed.

Unlike any other place in Alabama, Maxwell Field was integrated, meaning that the races were not kept apart. The President at the time, Franklin Roosevelt, had said that public places on military bases had to be open to black and white people equally.

Working at an integrated base meant that Rosa lived in a strange, divided world. During the workday, she could go anywhere she liked. She could drink from any water fountain. She could use any restroom. She could sit at any table in the cafeteria, even if a white person were sitting there. At the end of the day, she could take any seat on the trolley car that took workers to the edge of the base.

Rosa remembered those trolley rides all her life. She often described how she would sit up front, near a white co-worker and her nine-year-old son. The three of them would chat as they rode along. But when they reached the edge of the military base, they went back into a segregated world. They would pay the same fare and climb onto the same city bus. But while the little boy and his mother took seats up front, Rosa walked to the rear of the bus, where the "colored section" was. "The little boy would be looking at me so strangely," she remembered. Every day, she found going to the back of the bus a little more humiliating.

In her free time, Rosa had begun attending meetings of the Montgomery NAACP. There she met E.D. Nixon, the head of the group. Nixon reminded Rosa of her grandfather, and she liked him right away. Soon she was working as Nixon's volunteer secretary. She would take notes at meetings, write letters, and arrange for speakers to come.

Rosa soon became even more involved, as the advisor to the NAACP Youth Council. Rosa and Parks weren't able to have children of their own, but

Rosa loved working with black teens. She took them on field trips and taught them about black history.

Some of Rosa's other duties were less pleasant. She often went to interview black people who were the victims of race-based crimes. The NAACP wanted records of these crimes, hoping to encourage the victims to testify in court. Rosa heard horrible stories of lynchings, rapes, and attacks by white mobs. It hurt her to hear such terrible things, but she knew it was important for the stories to come out.

One of the NAACP's major efforts was to make it easier for black people to register to vote. The year she turned 30, in 1943, Rosa made it her goal to become registered. She knew it wouldn't be easy, and she was right. The process took two years.

First, Rosa had to find a time to go to the registration office. The office had no regular schedule. When it was open, it was usually only for two hours on a weekday morning. This was to make it difficult for black people with jobs to get there.

Finally, the office was open on Rosa's day off. She took the registration test. The white clerk who scored it told her that she had failed. It didn't do any good to ask why. The clerk didn't have to answer.

But Rosa didn't give up. She went back and took the test again. This time, she made a copy of the 21 questions and her answers. There were no copy machines in those days, so she wrote the copy out by hand. If she was told that she had failed again, she was going to use her copy to file a lawsuit against the registration board.

But this time, she was told she passed. At the age of 32, Rosa Parks was finally registered to vote in the state of

Alabama.

It was during one of her trips to the voter registration office that Rosa first encountered the bus driver, James Blake, who would play such a key role in her life—and in history—12 years later.

CHAPTER 8

The city buses in Montgomery contained 36 seats. By law, the first ten seats were reserved for white passengers. Even if there were no white people on the bus, a black person couldn't sit on one of those seats.

The last ten seats were reserved for black passengers. That left sixteen seats in the middle of the bus. It was up to the bus driver to decide how to divide those seats between whites and blacks. The drivers were all white men. They carried guns. When it came to enforcing segregation on a bus, the driver's word was law.

Not all bus drivers acted ugly towards their black passengers. But many did. And James Blake was one of the ugly ones.

Blake was driving the bus that Rosa boarded on her way to the registration office. The back of the bus was full. Black passengers were even standing on the outer steps at the rear of the bus.

Rosa paid her fare, then began walking down the aisle to the rear. But James Blake said, "Get off the bus and go in through the back door." He wouldn't even allow a black person to walk through the white seating area.

Rosa saw how crowded the back entrance was. Still standing in the aisle, she calmly told him it didn't make sense for her to leave the bus and try to push her way through that crowd.

Blake said, "Then you'll have to get off my bus."

Rosa did not move. She just stood there, calm and dignified.

Blake left his seat. He walked back to Rosa, grabbed her coat sleeve, and led her to the front door. There was an empty seat by the door. Rosa dropped her purse. Instead of just leaning over to get it, she sat on the "white" seat to pick it up.

"Get off my bus," Blake said. He was growing angrier.

"I will get off," Rosa replied. Blake was a tall, strong man. By now he was leaning over her in a threatening way. His fists were clenched. Rosa did not look afraid. She did not raise her voice. She just said, in a quiet, clear voice, "I know one thing. You better not hit me."

With those words, Rosa stood up and left the bus. She did not go to the rear entrance. She walked away to wait for another bus. As she did so, she told herself to watch out for James Blake in the future. She did not want to ever ride on his bus again.

Of course, she *would* end up on his bus again, on December 1, 1955. But this time, unlike their first meeting in 1943, she would not yield to his demands. When James Blake told her to move to the back of the bus, she simply refused, despite his threat to call the police.

CHAPTER 9

And so on that fateful December day, Blake called the police, and Rosa Parks was arrested.

Rosa didn't look much like a criminal. When the police arrived, they were not happy to find a neatly dressed, soft-spoken, 42-year-old lady. One of the officers seemed downright uncomfortable arresting her. "But the law is the law," he said.

She was taken to the city hall to be booked, and then to the city jail. From there, she called her home and spoke to her mother. "I'm in jail," she said calmly. "See if Parks will come down here and get me out." Her husband grabbed the phone. "Have they hurt you? Are you all right?" he asked.

By the time Rosa made her phone call, the word of her arrest was already spreading through the black community. Someone called E.D. Nixon, the head of the local NAACP. His wife told him, "You won't believe it. The police got Rosa. She's in jail." Nixon called a white attorney who worked with the NAACP. He, the attorney, and Parks all arrived at the jail at the same time. They paid her bail, and Rosa was released.

The four of them—Rosa, Parks, Nixon, and the white attorney, Clifford Durr—sat up late that night talking. In 1954, the United States Supreme Court, which makes the final decision on laws in the country, had ruled in the case of *Brown vs. the Board of Education* that school segregation was illegal. Ever since then, the four of them had been hoping to find an equally good case to challenge the laws on segregation in hotels, restaurants, libraries and other public places. They decided that buses would be a good place to start. And they realized that Rosa's case was just the one they had been waiting for.

They discussed something else, too. They wanted people talking about this case. They wanted the whole nation, not just Alabama, watching what was happening.

CHAPTER 10

Rosa and her allies came up with a dramatic idea. To protest Rosa's arrest and the laws about segregated buses, they would ask the black people of Montgomery to boycott—refuse to use—the city buses the following Monday, the day of Rosa's trial. Many more black people than white people used the city buses. If the black people didn't ride, the buses would be nearly empty.

The idea spread like wildfire. Volunteers printed thousands of leaflets that told about Rosa's arrest. The leaflets were taken door to door in the black community. They ended with the request, "Please stay off all buses on Monday."

That Sunday morning, black preachers announced the boycott in their churches. One young preacher became especially involved in organizing the boycott. His name was Martin Luther King, Jr. He was only 26 years old at the time.

Dr. King was not yet a famous man. He was a newcomer to Montgomery. But as soon as he heard the story of Rosa Parks and her arrest, he threw himself wholeheartedly into her case.

The people listened to Dr. King and the other preachers. They were fed up with being treated as second-class citizens. Many of them knew and respected Rosa and Parks. And on Monday morning, the buses of

Montgomery had only a handful of riders. The now-famous Montgomery Bus Boycott had begun!

Rosa's trial took place that afternoon. The courtroom was packed. Hundreds of supporters stood outside. When Rosa arrived, she looked like the dignified lady she was. She had on a black dress with white collar and cuffs and a small black velvet hat. She wore white gloves and carried a black purse. Watching her small figure approach the courthouse, one young girl called out, "Oh, she's so sweet! They messed with the wrong one now."

Rosa's trial lasted only thirty minutes. She was found guilty of breaking the segregation laws and fined fourteen dollars. That was more than half of her weekly salary.

Rosa's supporters were not upset about the verdict. Everyone knew that she would be found guilty. They *needed* her to be found guilty. Now they could take her case out of Montgomery and all the way to the Supreme Court.

That night, a meeting was held at the biggest black church in town. About five thousand people showed up. They spilled out of the church and into the yard and parking lot. Loudspeakers had to be set up so that everyone could hear.

As Rosa sat nearby, Martin Luther King, Jr., spoke to the crowd. In the rush of the day, Dr. King had almost no time to prepare a speech. Instead of relying on notes, he had to speak from his heart. This is part of what he said:

"My friends, I want it to be known that we're going to work with grim and firm determination to gain justice on the buses in this city. And we are not wrong. We are not wrong in what we are doing. If we are wrong, then the Constitution of the United States is wrong. If we are wrong, then God Almighty is wrong. If

*we are wrong, justice is a lie. And we are
determined in Montgomery to work and
fight until justice runs down like water
and righteousness like a mighty stream
. . ."*

When Dr. King finished speaking,
the crowd rose to their feet and
applauded for fifteen minutes. They
voted to continue the boycott—for as
long as it took to get justice.

Justice took a year. The Montgomery
Bus Boycott became known as one of
the most amazing events in American
history—an incredibly courageous act of
"civil disobedience." For a solid year, the
30,000 black citizens of Montgomery
stayed off the buses. In rain, in cold, in
steaming heat, they refused to give in.

Those who owned cars helped by
giving other people rides. Other people
traveled by bicycle. Some used carts
pulled by horses or mules.

But most walked. Day after day,

week after week, month after month—the buses were empty as the black people walked. They walked to school. They walked to church. They walked to work. And afterward, they walked home.

Day after day, word of what the people of Montgomery were doing spread across the nation and beyond. Photographs of the boycott were seen around the world. Television news crews came to interview the walkers. Newspapers published stories about the brave black Americans who were saying, "We will no longer be treated like second-class citizens."

The boycott embarrassed the city councilmen of Montgomery. They offered to add some buses that would be for blacks only. The boycotters said no. Police looked for excuses to arrest the boycotters. Racists threw bricks and rotten eggs at the black people walking by. But none of it made a difference.

The boycott would continue until Rosa Parks, and all black people, got justice.

The year of the boycott was not an easy time for Rosa and her family. She lost her job when her boss said there wasn't enough work for her. Parks was still barbering at Maxwell Field. His boss told him that he could keep his job—as long as he never mentioned Rosa or the boycott. Rather than agreeing, Parks quit. Rosa's mother, who lived with them, was elderly and not well. Rosa worried that the stress would harm her. And Rosa herself received letters and phone calls from people threatening to kill her. "This is all your fault," they said. "You deserve to die."

But on December 20, 1956, the boycott ended. The Supreme Court of the United States voted. It ruled that segregated buses, just like segregated schools, were illegal. The Court said that in Montgomery, as in every other city in the United States, blacks must be given the same rights on city buses as whites.

The boycotters knew that this decision would go far beyond the buses. The system of segregation was crumbling. By refusing to give up her seat, one woman had changed the lives of millions. Rosa Parks had changed history.

CHAPTER 11

The boycott was over. The buses were integrated. And Rosa Parks was known worldwide as "the mother of the civil rights movement."

If only good things happened to good people, the rest of Rosa's story would read like a fairy tale. She would live happily ever after, surrounded by the people who loved and respected her.

But Rosa's life after the boycott was no fairy tale. It was often difficult and, sometimes, even tragic.

Neither Rosa nor Parks could find

a job in Montgomery. Even people who supported Rosa were afraid to hire her. She had been labeled a "troublemaker." Employers didn't want their businesses to become the target of angry segregationists.

Even worse, some old friends from the civil rights movement were not kind to Rosa. They were jealous of the attention she received. They felt that their hard work on the boycott was not recognized. They said spiteful things to her: "Oh, here's the superstar. Are you sure you still have time for us?"

For a shy person like Rosa, who had never wanted attention, these remarks hurt badly. Less than a year after the boycott ended, Rosa, Parks, and Rosa's mother left Montgomery. They moved to Detroit, Michigan, where Rosa's brother Sylvester was living.

In Detroit, Rosa went to work in a factory, sewing aprons. Later, she was hired to work for John Conyers, a black congressman.

In 1968, when she learned that Martin Luther King, Jr. had been murdered in Memphis, Tennessee, Rosa was heartbroken. The killing seemed to be the beginning of years of trouble. She broke her ankle and wrist in a fall. By the mid-1970s, her husband, her brother, and her mother were all suffering from cancer. On many days, Rosa went to three different hospitals to spend time with her loved ones. Parks died in 1977. Three months later, Sylvester died as well. And Rosa's mother, Leona, died in 1979 at the age of 91.

Rosa retired from Representative Conyers' office when she was 74. Six years later, a man broke into her apartment and beat and robbed her. During the attack, he recognized her. He asked, "Aren't you Rosa Parks?" But he hit her and took her money anyway.

Most painful to Rosa was the fact that her attacker was a young black man. She told reporters after the incident, "I pray for him."

But there were wonderful moments in Rosa's later life as well. At the age of 80, she traveled outside the United States for the first time in her life, giving a speech to university students in Japan. When South African President Nelson Mandela, who had spent 27 years in prison for fighting against racism, visited the United States, Rosa was the person he most wanted to meet. President Bill Clinton honored her with a Medal of Freedom. And in Montgomery, a long, pleasant street bears the name "Rosa Parks Boulevard."

Rosa Parks died at the age of 92 in her Detroit apartment. Several close friends were with her at the end. In death, she received a great honor. Her coffin was placed inside the U.S.

Capitol building in Washington, D.C. Until that time, only presidents and great war heroes had "lain in state" at the Capitol. Thousands of mourners, both government officials and ordinary citizens, filed by the coffin to pay their last respects. She was buried with her husband and mother in Detroit.

And on the day of her funeral, in Montgomery, Alabama, the city of her great struggle and great triumph, the front seats of the city buses were empty. All the day's riders, black and white, took back seats in memory of Rosa Parks.

If you liked
***Rosa Parks*,**
you may be interested
in other true stories
in the Townsend Library.

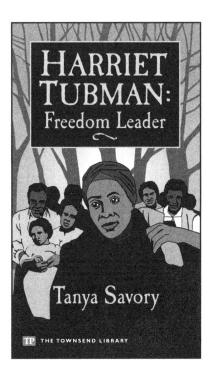

continued on the following pages

MARTIN LUTHER KING JR.

WARRIOR FOR PEACE

TANYA SAVORY

TP THE TOWNSEND LIBRARY

A DREAM FULFILLED
★ The Story of Barack Obama ★

TANYA SAVORY

TP THE TOWNSEND LIBRARY

Everyday Heroes

Beth Johnson

TP THE TOWNSEND LIBRARY

Letters My Mother Never Read:

AN ABANDONED CHILD'S JOURNEY

MOTHER OF 5 DIES IN TRAILER FIRE

By
JERRI DIANE SUECK

TP THE TOWNSEND LIBRARY

Visit us at www.townsendpress.com